Original title:
Whale Tales and Ocean Dreams

Copyright © 2025 Creative Arts Management OÜ
All rights reserved.

Author: Levi Montgomery
ISBN HARDBACK: 978-1-80587-362-4
ISBN PAPERBACK: 978-1-80587-832-2

Mysteries Beneath the Surface

Bubbles rise like whispered songs,
Where fish wear hats and swim along.
Seashells gossip in a wavy spree,
Jellyfish jesters dance with glee.

An octopus juggles seaweed snacks,
While crabs in costumes plot their tracks.
A sunken ship plays hide and seek,
With treasure chests that softly squeak.

The Dance of Giant Shadows

Inky giants glide with flair,
In a game of tag, they don't much care.
They twirl and spin, a watery show,
With a splash and a grin, they steal the show.

Turtles breakdance on the sandy floor,
While seahorses giggle and ask for more.
The whole wide ocean joins the fun,
With creatures laughing 'til the day is done.

Fluid Fantasies

A mermaid chuckles at a passing shark,
While dolphins leap and hit their mark.
They trade their stories of the sea,
In a goofy dance of harmony.

Starfish play cards on a sandy mat,
While a grouchy crab huffs and chats.
They all agree, life's a quirk,
In the ocean depths, where wonder works.

Breath of the Deep

Anemones tickle the floating air,
With giddy fish flopping everywhere.
A clam plays cards with a wise old eel,
Over secrets that the waves conceal.

Plankton parties under the moon,
Singing silly songs with a cheerful tune.
Every splash echoes laughter's call,
In the abyss where creatures frolic and sprawl.

The Dance of Unfathomable Giants

In azure depths, they twist and twirl,
With flippers flapping in a swirling whirl.
They wear top hats and dance like a fool,
A ballet of blubber in the ocean's pool.

Giant fish with shades, they groove to the beat,
Two barnacles join for a whimsical treat.
With jellyfish jelly as their fancy snack,
They spin like a top, then take a fun crack.

Beneath the Celestial Seafoam

Bubbles popping like popcorn afloat,
A turtle wearing glasses steers his small boat.
Starfish give high fives while dancing along,
As the waves carry whispers of a silly song.

A seahorse giggles, tickles a crab,
Who stumbles and tumbles, oh what a blab!
The dolphins crack jokes with a splash and a jump,
As the seaweed wiggles with every good thump.

Journey to the Coral Kingdom

In a kingdom where colors meld and bloom,
An octopus juggles his colorful loom.
He swaps out his hats for a dragonfly crown,
While schools of bright fish swim upside down.

A clam playing trumpet, so proud and loud,
Calls forth the jellyfish, who dance in a crowd.
With crabs doing cartwheels and clowns in the reef,
It's a circus in currents beyond belief!

Fantasies Beneath the Nautical Veil

Mermaids play chess with pirates on sand,
In shades of wild colors, they happily stand.
With treasure maps leading to ice cream delight,
They giggle and wiggle in the pale moonlight.

A narwhal in slippers serves drinks on a tray,
To octopus bartenders who sway and display.
They laugh at the moon as it winks in the sea,
In this bubble of humor, wild and carefree.

The Siren's Secret

A mermaid with a toothy grin,
Her fishy friends all gather in.
They sing a tune that's quite absurd,
While dolphins laugh at every word.

With jellyfish that dance and twirl,
A crab who thinks it's quite the girl.
Shells whisper secrets, salty drips,
While seaweed wears her finest flips.

Tidal Fantasia

The waves compose a wacky song,
As seagulls laugh and glide along.
A starfish plays the ukulele,
While clams keep time in their own way.

A sea cucumber joins the fun,
In a bubble bath, oh what a run!
Octopuses juggle, what a sight,
Under the moon, oh what delight!

A Canvas of Water Stories

An octopus with paint-stained arms,
Creates fine art that shares its charms.
With splashes bright, a fish parade,
A canvas made where dreams are laid.

A crab critiques, but can't decide,
On watercolor waves that ride.
While flounders giggle in their place,
At mismatched strokes that show their grace.

The Rhythm of Oceanic Breaths

The fish all dance in synchronized,
While waves move in a giggly rise.
A sea turtle wears funky shades,
And leads the crew in silly parades.

A lobster clicks its claws with cheer,
As turtle spins, "Come join me here!"
The bubble streams will make you grin,
In this big ocean, your fun begins!

Guardians of the Abyss

In the deep where bubbles pop,
A giant fish does belly flop.
With a splash and a giddy squeal,
He juggles anchors, what a deal!

A crab debates with a friendly ray,
"I swear I've seen you at the bay!"
They argue 'bout who's the better swimmer,
While the octopus paints with a shimmer!

A turtle spins like a dizzy top,
While seahorses laugh and hop.
The anglerfish turns off his light,
"Can we party all day and night?"

A clam sings tunes quite off-key,
While mermaids dance, oh so free.
The treasures glimmer, the laughs remain,
In this world beneath the waves' domain.

Echoes of the Midnight Sea

Bubbles rise like giggles in air,
As dolphins plot a game of dare.
With rubber noses, they jump and dive,
Making wishes to feel alive.

A shark in shades joins the fun,
"Don't be scared, I'm just a pun!"
He swims in circles, doing tricks,
While clownfish scold him for the mix.

Anchors drag the sleepy crew,
They sing of dreams, both old and new.
A starfish claims he knows a tale,
About the time he stole a pail!

When tides turn and laughter flies,
The sea becomes a canvas wide.
In midnight tunes, all creatures cheer,
Echoes of joy, a harmony near.

Chasing Shadows on the Shore

On sandy banks where shadows play,
Crabs wear hats and prance away.
They dance to music from the sea,
And try to be as quick as can be.

A seagull shrieks with cheeky glee,
"Come join the fun, it's free for thee!"
He drops a chip for a hungry fish,
Who jumps and flops, fulfilling wish!

With starfish at the limbo line,
They twist and sway, oh, how they shine.
A jellyfish juggles swimming shoes,
"Oh dear, will they fit? I've got the blues!"

As sunsets spill their vibrant hues,
The ocean giggles with funny cues.
With shadows chasing every sway,
The shore's a theater where all play.

Sailor's Lullaby Under Starlit Skies

Under skies where twinkling shines,
Sailors hum in silly lines.
The sea's their stage, a jolly show,
With fish that steal the limelight glow.

A ship that squeaks when it sets sail,
Tells tales of blunders, how they fail.
A parrot squawks, "That's not the way!"
As laughter rides the waves in play.

The captain's hat is worn too tight,
He trips on ropes that twirl in flight.
With every tumble, a hearty laugh,
The ocean giggles, "What a gaffe!"

As starlit waves embrace the night,
All sailors dance in pure delight.
A lullaby of chuckles soar,
The sea's a friend, forevermore.

The Rhythms of the Pelagic Realm

In the depths where shadows prance,
Fish have parties, take a chance.
They'll wear hats, and dance about,
With jellyfish, they'll scream and shout.

Octopus juggles shells with ease,
While shrimp line up to take their tease.
The sea stars clap, a shellfish band,
Crabs on the floor, get up and stand.

A sea cucumber starts a trend,
Teaching fish how to befriend.
With a wink, they swirl and sway,
In this dance, who leads the way?

So come, dear friend, and join the fun,
In waters where the pranks are spun.
The rhythms of the deep-sea choir,
Will leave you laughing, never tires.

Hidden Stories of the Deep

Bubbles rise with tales of cheer,
A clam just told the joke, I hear.
The giddy tuna giggle fills,
As dolphins flip and share their thrills.

In coral castles, secrets hide,
A grouper wears a mustache wide.
He tells the guppy, 'Take my fin,
Let's sneak a peek where laughs begin.'

They spy on turtles at the feast,
With seaweed cakes, they munch and east.
The octopus, dressed like a king,
Plays royal pranks and starts to sing.

So gather 'round, my fishy friends,
These hidden stories never end.
In the currents so kind and deep,
Let's dive and swim, but do not creep.

Mysterious Malachite Depths

In malachite where wonders lie,
The sea creatures wink and pry.
They wear their colors bold and bright,
At night, they throw a dazzling light.

The angler fish says with a grin,
'Come take a look, oh, let's begin!'
They have a light show, quite a scene,
With flashing scales, they steal the evening.

A grumpy seabed, full of sand,
Declares, 'You hooligans, understand?'
Yet all around, they dance like fools,
Spreading giggles through ocean schools.

So swim with glee, don't hold your breath,
In mysterious depths, they laugh at death.
Let's swirl and twirl, the night is young,
In the ocean's bosom, songs are sung.

Under the Embrace of the Blue

Under azure skies so wide,
Fins are flapping with great pride.
A narwhal snaps a selfie quick,
While others jostle, funny trick.

The seaweed wiggles, sways with glee,
As fishy friends join in the spree.
A starfish plays the ukulele,
With tunes that make the sharks go, 'Hey!'

A porpoise jokes, 'What's up, fin?'
While turtles argue, 'Who let him in?'
But laughter echoes through the tide,
As bubbles burst with joy, we glide.

So here beneath the cerulean hue,
Join frolics where the fish are true.
Under the embrace of the deep blue sea,
Every wave whispering, 'Be silly, be free!'

The Ocean's Heartbeat

Bubbles rise with a giggle,
Fish dance in a wiggle,
A turtle in a top hat,
Struts by with a chitchat.

Starfish in a conga line,
Clams chuckle, feeling fine,
A shrimp plays the ukulele,
While dolphins splash, oh so daily!

The seaweed sways, it's a party,
Octopuses getting hearty,
With each wave, a silly cheer,
The ocean sings, loud and clear.

In this splash of salty glee,
Creatures laugh with wild decree,
The ocean's secrets now unfurl,
Under waves, the fun's a whirl.

Siren Serenade

Siren cries with a wink,
Fishy friends pour a drink,
A seahorse in polka dots,
Sips a seaweed tea in pots.

Eels are mixing up some tunes,
Singing softly 'neath the moons,
With grins so wide, they croon along,
To bubbles popping in the throng.

With every splash and giggle loud,
Crabs breakdance, drawing a crowd,
Anemones in neon shades,
Twirl and whirl in joyful parades.

Deep beneath where the light fades,
Jellyfish in floats, parades,
In a place of merry chase,
Ocean pals in a silly race.

Depths of Enchantment

In the depths where laughter's found,
Sardines spin round and round,
Anglerfish with a glow so bright,
Tells jokes in the deep of night.

Seahorses with capes of silk,
Drink their coffee with warm milk,
Barnacles making quite the mess,
In their shell, they hold success.

An octopus knits a cozy hat,
For a clam who feels quite flat,
Grouper grins with a spout of air,
Stealing the show with style and flair.

Bubbles tell tales of the past,
Whimsical dreams too wild to cast,
In the ocean, where giggles shine,
Enchantment flows like a perfect line.

Waves of Whimsy

Waves crash with a playful splash,
Seagulls dive for the fish stash,
Flip-flops fly like a drone,
In sandy castles, laughter's grown.

Crabs wearing shades strut their stuff,
While the dolphins call their bluff,
Off they go in a silly spree,
Rolling waves, as wild as can be.

Jellybeans drift on the tide,
Sailing on a candy ride,
Mermaids join in on the fun,
Splashing colors, everyone!

With every whirl and every twirl,
Life beneath, a joyous swirl,
The ocean holds its secrets tight,
Filled with laughter, pure delight.

Legends of the Water's Heart

In the depths of the wavy blue,
A fish wore a hat, quite askew.
He'd tell goofy tales, like a star,
Of mermaids who danced in a rusty old car.

With a wink and a giggle, they splashed around,
Bubbles of laughter were always found.
The octopus juggled, a sight to behold,
While seahorses waltzed, both brave and bold.

They played cards with crabs, in a game undersea,
While sharks served the drinks, with a splash of glee.
In this curious world of whimsy so grand,
The flip-flop fish danced to their own funky band.

Under the sea, where the currents sway,
The antics continue on a bright sunny day.
Legends are silly but filled with good cheer,
In the heart of the water, fun's always near.

The Siren's Call at Dusk

At twilight's glow, a call rang clear,
A siren with puns, she'd bring good cheer.
With a flick of her tail, she spun tales of old,
Of jellyfish parties, all brash and bold.

She sang of a crab who wore socks on his claws,
And a dolphin who dreamed of starring in jaws.
Shells laughed along with the starfish amazed,
As her stories grew more and delightfully crazed.

With tunes made of bubbles and splashes of fun,
They danced 'til the daylight, to night they would run.
The sea critters giggled, they turned in delight,
As they revelled in mischief under the moonlight.

Folk tales of fish who could tickle and tease,
Would echo and shimmer, carried on the breeze.
And in the soft dusk, they all would agree,
This siren of laughter, a true friend to be.

Driftwood Reveries

On a plank of driftwood, a crab took a seat,
With a map in his claws, he plotted his feat.
"Treasure!" he cheered, "with jewels so bright,
With gummy worms waiting, what a tasty sight!"

A pelican swooped, squawking out loud,
"There's a party ahead, come gather the crowd!"
Flipping through soggy old books made of kelp,
They laughed at the tales, till they cried, "Help, help!"

Stars overhead blinked in a jazzy parade,
As fish formed a line, for the conch-shell charade.
Driftwood turned stage, with antics galore,
As sardines performed with a slapstick encore.

With an audience made of sand dollars and more,
The giggles echoed from the shallow sea floor.
In splashes of whimsy, the night rolled away,
Driftwood reveries colored their play.

Secrets of the Celestial Tide

In the hush of the night, the sea whispered soft,
Of secrets and smart crabs, witty and aloof.
Orcas played chess with the stars overhead,
While lazy old turtles just dreamed in their bed.

They passed on the tales of a squid who could dance,
With moves like a pro, he took quite a chance.
Each flip and each spin brought shrieks of delight,
As dolphins would cheer, under the starlit night.

The clams formed a band, with shells made of gold,
Playing tunes that would sparkle, both bright and bold.
A symphony crafted from bubbles and foam,
In the marvel of magic, they felt quite at home.

So if you should paddle or drift in the tide,
Listen close to the laughter where sea spirits hide.
The secrets they share are a splendid delight,
In the ocean's embrace, where joy takes its flight.

Currents of Imagination

In a sea of bright idea fish,
They swim around with style and swish.
A dolphin wears a polka dot hat,
While turtles dance and have a chat.

Octopuses play poker in the sun,
Their tentacles deal, oh what fun!
A crab cracks jokes with a wink and a grin,
While mermaids giggle, tuning their fin.

Seahorses paint murals with a splash,
With colors vibrant, a coral mash.
They gather 'round for a silly song,
In the shallow waves, they all belong.

As currents twist in a playful flow,
New tales emerge where laughter will grow.
With every splash and bubble too,
Imagination sails, so bright and true!

Ripples of Forgotten Lore

Once a fish told tales of great delight,
How seashells can sing on a full moon night.
With grinning starfish as the audience,
Each story sparked laughter, none could convince.

An old whale claimed he danced with the tide,
But he tripped on kelp, and oh, how he cried!
Seagulls cackled, flapping their wings,
As plankton joined in with their tiny things.

The jellyfish flashed their disco lights,
While barnacles joined in, giving frights.
They rapped and they tapped, a watery show,
In ripples of lore, their stories flow.

As laughter echoes 'neath waves so bright,
Forgotten tales awaken in the night.
Through currents of fun, the ocean song,
In every wave, we all belong!

Swim with the Stars

Beneath the waves, where dreams take flight,
Fish twinkle like stars in the darkest night.
A school of sardines forms a gleaming line,
While sea turtles waltz, feeling just fine.

An anglerfish dressed in a tutu bright,
Leads a conga line in the moon's soft light.
They spin and they twirl, making quite a scene,
In the grand ball where no one is mean.

Starfish toss sparkles and giggle with glee,
While clownfish crack jokes, as silly as can be.
Their laughter rises like bubbles to the top,
In the vast blue, the good times never stop.

So come join the party, no stars left behind,
With fins all a-whirl, oh what fun you'll find!
In the ocean's embrace, let your spirit roam,
As we swim with the stars, forever home.

Legends of the Briny Deep

In the briny deep, where legends reside,
A squid told a tale with much ocean pride.
He claimed he found treasure, a chest full of gold,
But alas, it was seaweed, a sight to behold.

A grouper named Gary, quite hefty and round,
Said he'd once wrestled a shark that he found.
With tales of glory, he'd puff up with zest,
But the shark was just nibbling on some sea lettuce.

Crabs painted stories on the ocean floor,
With their pinchers and brushes, they never bore.
They crafted a mural of legends untold,
With laughter and color, their tales unfold.

Drifting along, the stories grew wide,
In the depths of the sea, we laugh and abide.
With every wave that brings us new cheer,
The legends of laughter are always near!

Adrift in Celestial Currents

A fish in a suit, oh what a sight,
Waltzing through bubbles, in sheer delight.
He asks for a dance, those bubbles comply,
While jellyfish giggle and wink from the sky.

A crab with a monocle, reading his map,
Left his sand castle, took quite a nap.
With tides doing tango, how could he fret?
He just makes a cocktail of seaweed and wet.

The octopus juggles, with flair and with style,
His eight arms are busy, he's quite the isle.
He shimmies and shakes, oh my, what a show,
As the sea turtles cheer, 'Look at him go!'

But wait, out of nowhere, a dolphin appears,
Wearing a top hat, and crying with cheers.
"Let's surf on a wave, with style and with grace!"
As crabs clap their claws, it's a bubbly embrace.

The Majesty Below

In the depths of blue, a conga line starts,
With fish in a frenzy, and all of their arts.
A squid with a sax, playing tunes that enchant,
While the sharks shake their fins, doing polka and chant.

A clam pulls a prank, with pearls on a string,
He teases a grouper, who wears quite a bling.
"Why do you swagger?" the grouper replies,
"Because I'm a starfish, with ten thousand eyes!"

The coral becomes a grand stage in the sea,
As starfish spin tales of how funny they be.
With laughter erupting, the seaweed sways,
It's a circus of life, in the ocean's displays.

But watch out, here comes a whale with a grin,
He's taken up acting, much to his chagrin.
But his role as a dragon, is simply a blast,
With a splash and a wink, he's the ocean's contrast.

Tidal Whispers

The tides whisper secrets, float light as a breeze,
While anemones giggle with glee and with tease.
A starfish with shades, soaking rays on the sand,
He scrolls through his findings, the ocean so grand.

The seahorse plans picnics, with seashells for chairs,
He invites all his friends, with laughter to share.
"Don't eat too much plankton, or you'll float away!"
The sardines all chuckle, "We'll be here all day!"

A bubble appears, with a joke in its core,
It pops with a chuckle, who could ask for more?
Dolphins, they leap, and they dive with much charm,
As the octopus teases, "Come join in, don't be a harm!"

But the tides keep on speaking, a chatter, a hum,
With whispers of laughter and joy they become.
In the ocean's embrace, with a wink and a sway,
The dance of the deep, where the silly hold sway.

Embrace of the Marine Compass

Beneath a bright surface, where currents collide,
A compass of laughter, where fishies reside.
With turtles and dolphins, all in pursuit,
The treasure's a giggle, all wrapped in a boot.

A shrimp in a sailor's cap, shouting with pride,
"Who lost the map? Let's just ride with the tide!"
A crab waves his claws, with sass and with flair,
"Let's set sail for giggles, not treasure or wear!"

With seaweed for ropes, they hoist up a sail,
While the fish crack jokes like they're on a grand trail.
"Are we there yet?" they ask, with a flip and a spin,
And the seagulls just cackle, "Oh please, let's begin!"

In this remarkable voyage, the humor's the key,
For in every small wave, is giggles set free.
As the ocean sings songs of joy and of fun,
They embrace all the tides, under a great shining sun.

Tranquil Tales from the Foam

In waters deep where laughter gleams,
A fish wore glasses, or so it seems.
It swam with style, a real great show,
Telling stories of tides long ago.

A crab with a hat danced on the rocks,
Singing loud tunes that tickled the flocks.
Octopuses joined in, quite the affair,
Jiving and jiving without any care.

Bubbles floated, catching the sun,
Each little pop, a giggle, a pun.
Seahorses giggled, rode fish like bikes,
Jumping around like silly old tykes.

With fins in the air and tails in a twist,
Every moment a splash, none could resist.
The ocean's a party, wild and bright,
Where laughter and waves meet, pure delight.

The Depths of Dreamers

In a kelp forest where shadows play,
A starfish proclaimed it was his birthday.
All the sea urchins threw him a bash,
With jellyfish dancing in colorful flash.

A dolphin swirled, wearing a crown,
Claiming the title of the Ocean's clown.
While fish threw confetti, oh what a sight,
Even the crabs clapped with all their might.

With balloons made of bubbles, they swam in a line,
Singing sea shanties, sipping on brine.
A narwhal juggled shells as they cheered,
In this underwater fest, no one was feared.

The tides whispered secrets, waves rolled with glee,
As all joined together in pure jubilee.
Delightful abounds in the salt-scented air,
Where dreams of the ocean spark laughter to share.

Chasing the Horizon's Echo

Two turtles decided to race one fine day,
With seaweed as flags, they galloped away.
Bubbles flew high, and laughter erupted,
As they flipped through waves, quite uncorrupted.

A starry-eyed seagull cheered them along,
Squawking out melodies, oh so wrong.
He mixed up the tunes, but it was alright,
For every off-note brought more delight.

The finish line? Just a rock with a shell,
Where crabs distracted them with tales to tell.
"Did you see that wave?" squeaked a clam in its shell,
"Last week, I rode it and lived to tell!"

In a splash of mischief, they all took a dive,
In the heart of the ocean, so lively, alive.
Each wave was a giggle, each current a tease,
As the turtles discovered the joy of the seas.

Oceanic Reveries

Moray eels giggled in cozy nest beds,
Swapping wild stories with seaweed for threads.
A whale had a party, their tunes sailed so far,
Beached on a carpet of soft-looking tar.

Chasing the bubbles, the plankton all danced,
Fish painted faces, oh how they pranced!
A tuna with maracas shook to the beat,
While shrimp formed a line, tapping their feet.

They twirled and they swirled in underwater rows,
While dolphins filmed antics for future shows.
With cameras of shells, twinkling they spun,
Giggles and splashes, oh what a fun run!

As daylight shimmered, the fun must recede,
In the depths of the oceans, joy takes a lead.
With whimsical tales and a heart full of play,
The sea dreams alive in a splashy display.

Beneath the Silver Gleam

In the depths a fish wore a hat,
Said, "I'm the king of this fine habitat!"
A crab in a tux looked quite dapper,
They danced on the sand with a joyful clapper.

The octopus juggled his shiny pearls,
While singing a tune that made fishes twirl.
A dolphin with shades, thought he was so cool,
He tried to teach stingrays how to play pool.

A turtle in flip-flops strolled down the lane,
While a seagull shouted, "Come join the fun train!"
The seaweed laughed at the silly parade,
In this underwater escapade!

With bubbles and giggles, they splashed all about,
The ocean's a circus, no shadow of doubt!
Beneath the silver gleam, they frolicked so free,
In a world bursting bright, as funny as can be!

Odyssey of the Deep Blue

A clam with a dream of becoming a star,
Wore sunglasses and said, "I'll go far!"
The jellyfish giggled, floating on by,
"With moves like yours, you'll just need to try!"

The sea horse spun like a ballerina,
While seaweed waved like a grand ballerina.
Anemone joined in, shaking its sleeves,
The laughter echoed through corals and leaves.

A grouper planned parties with pom-poms and cheer,
While shrimps whispered secrets for all to hear.
The eel told a joke, though it was quite shocking,
Even the starfish were caught belly-laughing!

As bubbles danced up to the bright ocean light,
The tales of the deep spun a tapestry bright.
An odyssey filled with chuckles and glee,
Where water's sweet laughter is flowing free!

Mariner's Moonlight Narrative

By the moonlight, the otters played tag,
Chasing each other with giggles that brag.
A narwhal wiggled his long pointed horn,
Claiming he'd been to the world's fashion dawn!

The fish had a feast with a berry pie slice,
While the crabs served drinks that tasted quite nice.
A sea cucumber swayed with a wink and a grin,
Saying, "This party should never begin!"

The turtles told tales of the high seas they knew,
Of daring escapes and some wild ocean blues.
The laughter rolled in with the waves like a song,
As waves crested high, it all felt so wrong!

With starfish clapping in rhythm so sweet,
The ocean's delight felt quite silly repeat.
In the mariner's moonlight, with joy and a cheer,
They partied all night till dawn's light drew near!

The Siren's Soliloquy

In a bubble of giggles, a siren did sing,
With a voice that could charm any curious thing.
She braided her hair with some seaweed and shells,
While fish danced around, casting whimsical spells.

"Oh, how I love when the sailors come near,
They bring me adventures and stories to hear!"
The lobsters joined in with their claws held up high,
"We'll catch all the laughs and let them fly!"

A dolphin chimed in, also aiming to please,
"I've traveled the seas with the greatest of ease!"
And while they all giggled, a whale in disguise,
Made bubbles that painted the brightest starry skies.

So beneath the waves in this world full of fun,
The siren laughed loud, her heart like a sun.
In her soliloquy of joy and delight,
Together they danced through the endless night!

Whispers of the Aquatic Realm

In the depths where the fishes play,
A dolphin laughs at a crab's ballet.
Octopuses juggle with style and grace,
As seaweed wiggles, tickling their face.

A turtle's slow, but his jokes are fast,
He tells a tale, oh, what a blast!
Starfish chiming in with a wink,
"We might be crusty, but we sure can think!"

The squids are dancing, ink in the air,
While clownfish giggle without a care.
A party of bubbles is coming in soon,
And everyone's hoping to burst like a balloon!

With giggles and splashes, who thought we'd find,
That laughter abounds in the sea, unconfined?
So join the merriment, don't be a bore,
For life's just a splash, and there's always more!

The Harmony of Deep Waters

In the deep blue where laughter flows,
A grouper hums as the seaweed grows.
Fishes playing tag, oh what a sight,
They dart like bullets, quick, left, and right.

A whale with a hat sings off-key,
Calling for dolphins to dance with glee.
"Hey, two-step! Now do the twist!"
With fins in a whirl, they can't resist.

The clownfish sport a psychedelic hue,
Telling sea stories that just aren't true.
"Did you see the ship that went down with a boom?
I swear it was made of chocolate and gloom!"

With echoes of laughter rippling through,
The ocean's a stage where dreams come true.
So come for a swim, leave all your cares,
In the realm of silly oceanic affairs!

Beneath Starlit Waves

Beneath the stars, where the turtles scoot,
A fisherman's hat makes a fine parachute.
"Catch of the day!" yelled a mackerel with glee,
But it turns out, it's just a lost flip-flop, you see!

Glowfish glow while they tell ghostly tales,
About jellyfish sailors who once rode the gales.
"Do you think they found treasure or just a jelly snack?"
The wise sea cucumber hopes they're coming back!

A crab with sunglasses, all cool and relaxed,
Declares that his dance moves are complex and waxed.
"Try my moonwalk on sand—we'll sweep the floor!"
But the prawns just giggle and roll on the shore.

The moon dips low, a party in flight,
As fish join the chorus – all feeling just right.
So come touch the waves, let worries unwind,
In this ocean of laughter, true joy you will find!

Sailing through Liquid Dreams

Sailing through dreams on a jellyfish fleet,
With penguins in bowties, oh, what a treat!
They glide over bubbles, sip sea cucumber tea,
While a parrotfish cracks jokes by the sea.

An otter pulls pranks, with a wink and a flip,
"Who hid my ball? Was it you, little shrimp?"
The seahorses giggle, tails all entwined,
While starfish applaud from their spots, well-defined.

A mermaid croons softly, her voice like a bell,
She sings of the time that she tripped and fell.
"Got tangled in seaweed, fell right on my face,
But the fish all cheered, 'What a magical grace!'"

With laughter echoing through both currents and swells,
Each creature a comrade, with stories to tell.
So raise up your fins, let's glide with delight,
In this world of antics, we sail through the night!

Echoes of the Tides

In a splashy dance, fish wear hats,
Seahorses giggle, doing acrobat chats.
The octopus juggles, with eight arms free,
While crabs play poker beneath the sea.

A narwhal honks out a funny tune,
As dolphins dive, making waves like a cartoon.
The seaweed sways, joining in the fun,
Underwater laughter drowns out the sun.

Starfish throw parties on sandy floors,
While jellyfish glide, showing off their scores.
Anemones clap to the rhythm of waves,
As everyone jiggles, the ocean misbehaves.

At sunset's glow, they all take a breather,
Singing serenades to the whimsical ether.
In this watery world, joy never hides,
Where laughter bubbles up with the tides.

Guardians of the Abyss

In the deep blue, a turtle dons specs,
Surveying the sea like a quirky reflex.
With crusty old clams hearing gossip anew,
The creatures chuckle at tales that ensue.

A squid with a bowtie throws a ball,
While anchovies gather, getting ready to sprawl.
The eels do their best to wiggle and tease,
In this underwater realm, the antics never freeze.

A grumpy old grouper hums a sad song,
But the party of shrimps knows how to ping along.
They tickle the corals; the bubbles arise,
As everyone joins in with laughter and sighs.

In the depths of the sea, the guards wear their grins,
Keeping watch over laughter, where the real fun begins.
With each little giggle, they strengthen the ties,
In the watery kingdom, where humor can rise.

Leviathan's Lullaby

A giant with dreams of a shimmering moon,
Sings softly to fishes a sweet, sleepy tune.
With a belly so big, it rumbles with cheer,
While plankton float by without any fear.

The kraken plays peek-a-boo with the sun,
Leaping from shadows, just having some fun.
With tentacles waving like ribbons in air,
Creating a spectacle beyond compare.

A pufferfish giggles, full of hot air,
Turning into balloons, floating without care.
With a swarm of tiny shrimp dancing around,
They twirl in a frenzy, joyfully unbound.

As the moon whispers secrets to the waves,
The leviathan dreams, and the ocean behaves.
In this slumbering world, laughter remains,
While the currents carry both joy and refrains.

Murmurs of the Sea

In the shallows, a clam tells a joke to a snail,
While flounders play cards, trying hard not to fail.
A starfish giggles at a crab in a dance,
Swirling with laughter, giving fate a chance.

The sea cucumbers shimmer with glee,
As they form a conga line, just to be free.
With pearls in their shells, they shine and they sway,
Crafting sweet moments at the end of the day.

An otter floats by, juggling seaweed,
With laughter that echoes, like joy's very seed.
While sea turtles compete in a race filled with speed,
The ocean is buzzing with laughter indeed!

In this watery realm, the fun never stops,
With every splash growing, the joy only hops.
Where whispers and chuckles blend into a spree,
Murmurs of magic flow wild and carefree.

Echoing through the Waves

In the splash of the sea, there's a story to tell,
Where fish wear hats and dolphins ring a bell.
Octopus onstage, doing a jig,
While crabs clap their claws, dancing a big wig.

Sharks munching on tacos, a feast so bizarre,
While turtles are racing their shells in a car.
The seaweed sways, joins in the fun,
Underwater laughter, everyone's on the run.

Seahorses surfing on waves made of cream,
Starfish are juggling, living the dream.
A clam with a banjo, strumming a tune,
Sings "Under the Sea" by the light of the moon.

With each bubble burst, a giggle is shared,
In this wacky world, nobody's scared.
Just a zany parade in an oceanic spree,
Where the silliness flows, as wild as can be.

Odyssey of Ocean Giants

A big blue creature with a bowtie so grand,
Serves tea to the gulls with a wave of his hand.
Whales whisper secrets in bubbles of air,
While sea turtles park in a best-dressed affair.

Giant squids play chess with the fish on the side,
As otters hold court, the ocean's pride.
Jellyfish dancing with lights in their glow,
While crabs count the stars in a line, row by row.

With kraken's delight, they all take a ride,
On the back of a turtle, the ocean their guide.
They chat and they laugh in a whirlpool of glee,
As sea creatures gather for a grand jamboree.

Their tales mix with laughter, a watery song,
For in this deep world, everyone belongs.
So raise your fins high and join in the cheer,
For tales from the depths, where all hearts are clear.

Beneath the Horizon's Glimmer

A mermaid in shades, lounging with flair,
While fish-selling gossip floats through the air.
Seagulls wear shades, squawking wise quotes,
Navigating the waves in their tiny little boats.

Coral reefs bloom like a party gone wild,
As clownfish paint faces, so happy and styled.
They twirl and they spin, such a colorful sight,
Electric eels glow, lighting up the night.

With waves as their canvas, the ocean does sing,
As the conch shells echo, the joy that they bring.
Bubbles of laughter rise up to the blue,
Each ripple a giggle, a frolicsome crew.

Beneath the horizon where wonders combine,
The spirit of fun dances under the brine.
So come take a dive, in this whimsical stream,
Where every fin sways with laughter and gleam.

Celestial Beacons in the Deep

Starfish stargaze with eyes wide and bright,
Counting all the comets that shimmer at night.
Anemones giggle, tickled by tides,
While jolly sea creatures wear smiles that glide.

A narwhal with bling, glides through the dark,
With tales of the moon, and a very bright spark.
Eels in a conga line dance in a groove,
While fish throw confetti, making a move.

Even the octopus wears fancy new shoes,
Stomping and twirling, singin' the blues.
As currents swirl around, igniting their glee,
In this cosmic foam, where all hearts swim free.

With bioluminescent joy lighting the way,
They shoot for the stars and invite you to play.
So dive into the deep, where laughter does leap,
Among celestial beacons that twinkle and peep.

An Odyssey in Aquatic Realms

In the deep blue, fish do swim,
Chasing bubbles on a whim.
One tried to dance with a sock,
But ended up stuck on a rock.

Octopus juggling with seashells,
Crabs playing tag, oh, what fun spells!
A dolphin forgot how to leap,
And landed straight in a seaweed heap!

A turtle's slow race, what a sight,
He thought he'd win, but lost to a kite.
Seahorses giggling, a royal parade,
With crowns made of bubbles, a bubble charade!

As waves clap their hands like fans,
The ocean's got its funny plans.
So dive in, find laughter undone,
In this realm, we all are one!

Melodies from the Silent Depths

In the silence, fish hum a tune,
Dancing beneath a silver moon.
A clam tried to sing operatic notes,
But only splashed water from its throats.

The starfish shook, doing the twist,
While anemones said, "We've got the gist!"
A grouper looked lost in a swirling dance,
He stumbled right into a shrimp's romance!

Jellyfish jiggled with elegant grace,
While sea cucumbers held their place.
Their version of ballet, a wobbly feat,
Had everyone laughing, it couldn't be beat!

Echoing giggles from critter to critter,
Sound waves bounce, not one gets bitter.
In a world where the silly is true,
We dive deep for laughter, me and you!

Tales from the Coral Canvas

Coral reefs dressed in a rainbow hue,
Fish dabbing paint, oh what a view!
A parrotfish splattered with colors bright,
Said, "Artistic fish have a splash of delight!"

Clownfish trying to tell a joke,
But all they could do was croak and smoke.
A pufferfish puffed up with pride,
While a crab rolled his eyes and sighed.

Seahorses racing on tiny bikes,
Making bets with the sea's small spikes.
An octopus with eight paintbrushes danced,
With a master stroke, the sea pranced!

With laughter blooming from reef to reef,
Creatures join in, casting aside grief.
In this canvas where colors blend,
Each tale spins joy, like a circle's end!

Mysterious Depths and Glittering Skies

In the depths where shadows play,
Squid shadows danced the night away.
With neon lights that flickered bright,
They twirled and swirled, what a sight!

A whale tried to do the moonwalk,
Made quite a splash and caused some talk.
A sunfish was caught in a fishing line,
Said, "I'm just checking, is this a sign?"

The starlight twinkled through watery trails,
While anglerfish told the best flails.
"Why did the crab never share his cake?"
"Because he had a shellfish mistake!"

The ocean echoed with laughter loud,
As bubbles gathered a glittering crowd.
So dive into fun, let the laughter rise,
In these playful depths and glittering skies!

The Current's Gentle Touch

Bubbles rise and fish make faces,
Seaweed dances in funny places.
Crabs wear hats, what a sight to see,
Shuffling sideways, doing a jig in glee.

A dolphin's laugh might make you snicker,
While turtles shuffle, getting quicker.
Starfish giggle as they flip and flop,
With each wave, they just can't stop.

The jellyfish bounces with a glow,
Tickling each fish, putting on a show.
Seahorses waltz with silly grace,
In the currents' embrace, they all find their place.

From the depths to the coral's edge,
Ocean creatures make a fun pledge.
To dance and sing through day and night,
In the playful realm of the sea, pure delight.

Nightfall Over the Azure Embrace

As the sun dips down, the stars appear,
The fish all gather, oh what a cheer!
Octopus juggling with a grin so wide,
Under the moon, they dance, they glide.

Cranky old seagulls stealing snacks,
Watch out for tides, they sneak on tracks!
Anglerfish casting light so bright,
Pulling pranks in the dim night light.

Shells play music while the swell is low,
Prawns in tutus put on a show.
The crabs are scuttling, full of pride,
With every wave, they ride, they slide.

Bubbles pop and laughter echoes loud,
The sea is filled with a giggling crowd.
As night drapes over the ocean's sweep,
In this watery world, there's joy to keep.

Serenade of the Sea Creatures

Turtles croon in their shellish way,
Fish form a choir, ready to play.
With bubbles rising, they start the beat,
Clapping fins, oh what a treat!

The squid shake it on the sandy floor,
While little shrimp tap dance to score.
Guitar crabs strum with claws so fine,
Creating tunes under the ocean's shine.

Sea cucumbers sway, a bit out of time,
But don't you worry, they're having a prime.
Sea stars sway in a calm ballet,
While the mackerel twirl in a flashy display.

In this concert of the brine and blue,
Every creature has a role to do.
So join their fun and sway along,
In the ocean's embrace, they all belong.

Portraits of the Dark Abyss

Down in the depths, where the light won't creep,
Creatures gather as the shadows leap.
Anglerfish smile with a glittery lure,
While deep-sea monsters make you unsure.

Blobfish at parties, such a strange sight,
Trying to dance in the pale moonlight.
With unruly hair and a zany grin,
They flip and flop, like they're born to spin.

Those sea spiders boast such crazy legs,
Trying to woo the dark with their pegs.
In this abyss, where jokes abound,
Hilarity swims all around.

So let's raise a glass to the creatures below,
In the depths of the seas where the weirdos flow.
In the dark, they laugh, and do their dance,
Making the most of their curious chance.

The Pulse of the Untamed

In the depths where blubbers play,
A fish tried to tango, but swam away.
Sea cucumbers giggled in the sand,
While octopuses juggled, quite unplanned.

A crab wore a hat, oh what a sight,
Claiming the beach as his rightful right.
Starfish spoke gossip, sharing the news,
Of clams in their shells with terrible blues.

Gentle giants danced, flukes in the air,
Singing to dolphins without a care.
Seagulls quacked jokes about barnacle glue,
While turtles shared tales that simply weren't true.

Mollusks in slippers, quite chic they seemed,
Chased after bubbles, in laughter they dreamed.
The ocean's a party, come join the fun,
Where everyone's silly, and no one is done.

Ocean's Embrace

Bubbles burst forth in effervescent cheer,
As fish throw a bash for the ocean's frontier.
Jellyfish glow like disco balls bright,
While seaweed sways, dancing through the night.

Turtles in tuxedos strut down the reef,
Tripping on currents, no sign of grief.
Crabs in cool shades, looking so sly,
With jokes about clams that simply can't fly.

A dolphin named Dave led the conga line,
While snails brought cocktails, all salty and fine.
With laughter and splashes, they echoed around,
The ocean an echo of joy in the sound.

So dive in the splash, let the fun commence,
In this quirky world, life's a great suspense.
For under the waves, all is whimsy and glee,
Come swim with the creatures, so wild and so free!

Beneath Waves of Wonder

Beneath the surface, a party unfolds,
Fish in tuxedos spin tales quite bold.
Seahorses gallop, flapping their fins,
While barnacles giggle, and the fun never ends.

Anemones play hide and seek with the tide,
While colorful critters are bursting with pride.
Squids throw confetti, ink flying around,
As turtles groove to the rhythm of sound.

Pufferfish blow up, just for a laugh,
While mermaids take selfies, oh what a gaffe!
The ocean's a dance floor, so wild and absurd,
With jellyfish swirling, just following the herd.

Eels share their jokes while spinning in circles,
As lobsters crack puns like tricky old turtles.
With laughter and bubbles, it's quite a delight,
In the depths of the ocean, the party ignites!

A Voyage to Distant Shores

On a ship made of seaweed and glittery shells,
Sailed a brave captain who cast funny spells.
With fish as his crew, all dancing in line,
They set off to find a bright treasure divine.

A parrot named Polly was chief of the jest,
With tales of a treasure that was all but a quest.
He squawked of a fortune in lost rubber boots,
And gold-plated sea cucumbers wearing fine suits.

As waves tossed their boat, they giggled and roared,
In search of a treasure nobody adored.
With laughter like cannonballs, echoing free,
The crew knew that joy was their greatest decree.

Finally arriving on a strange sandy plot,
They dug up a treasure, it was all just a blot!
But smiles filled the deck; they had all that they sought,
For laughter and friendship are treasures untaught.

Ghosts of the Ocean's Past

Bubbles in the water, making quite a show,
A fish in top hat struts, with a twirling bow.
Seashells gossip softly, secrets they bestow,
While jellyfish remind us, that dancing's all for flow.

Pirates in their glory, with treasure chests so bright,
Chasing after sea cucumbers, what a funny sight!
A crab with a monocle, declares he's quite polite,
As octopuses juggle, under the moon's soft light.

Mermaids tell of rumors, of what the tides may bring,
Seagulls snicker boldly, on a ship with fish to swing.
Coconuts are laughing, never one to cling,
While starfish play the guitar, making the ocean sing.

A sea horse in a race, with a dolphin on his tail,
While snails make sure to cheer, none are destined to fail.

A squirt of sea foam giggles, with every mischievous gale,

As the ocean holds its laughter, in this hilarious tale.

Chimeras of Coral Reefs

Amongst bright coral castle, a turtle wears a crown,
Puffers tell a tall tale, about a fish who drowned.
Parrots squawk the jokes right, echoing all around,
While clownfish are the comedians, with laughter they astound.

The urchins hold a fiesta, their spikes adorned in flair,
Dancing with the anemones, waving in the air.
A crab's got jokes for days, with a pinch of loving care,
Beneath the sea's grand ballroom, no one has a despair.

Angelfish are flirting, hiding in the reef's embrace,
As sardines form a conga, in a synchronized race.
The seahorses are spinning, with elegance and grace,
Creating rhythms Ocean-wide, ready to leave a trace.

The starfish are the judges, on a thrumming stage of sand,

As laughter swells and echoes, across this magic land.
With every gentle wave, they dance in seas so grand,
A colorful parade, which none could ever withstand.

A Journey Through Salted Dreams

Once upon a wave, where silliness does dwell,
A narwhal with a banjo, sings a quirky spell.
Tuna slice through bubbles, like a fishy carousel,
As seagrass sways to rhythms, in this ocean shell.

Dolphins crack the best jokes, riding high on swells,
While crustaceans gather 'round, pulling hilarious spells.
With seafoam mustaches, the beach parties compel,
To dance with octopus legs, in a watery hotel.

Caught inside a sea swirl, we float through wacky dreams,

Focused on the laughter, that's bursting at the seams.
We chase after the flicker, of phosphorescent gleams,
In this salty wonderland, where nothing's as it seems.

As we paddle toward the shore, the sun begins to rise,
With rainbow-colored seashells, hiding in disguise.
A final splash of laughter, as the seagull cries,
Our journey etched in memories, beneath the ocean skies.

Reflections on the Whispering Waters

In a boat made of jelly, we float with a grin,
Fish are our crew, let the antics begin!
A turtle in glasses is calling us near,
"Do you take cash or credit for seaweed and beer?"

Octopuses dance, with eight arms they sway,
Trading their secrets for some chips on the way.
We laugh at a crab who's caught in a net,
Shouting, "Don't worry, we all need a pet!"

The seagulls are gossiping, feathers afluff,
"Did you see that shark? His jokes are quite tough!"
With bathtubs as boats and sea cows as friends,
Our days are all wacky, the laughter never ends!

We roll with the waves, as the dolphins tease,
"Join us for a splash, we'll do it with ease!"
In waters of whimsy, we swim and we dive,
Floating on giggles, oh, how we survive!

Fantasia of Fluid Worlds

In a ballet of bubbles, the fish betake flight,
With pirouettes perfect, they dance day and night.
A crab with a top hat, he tips it with flair,
Says, "Join the fandango, if you're brave, if you dare!"

The sea cucumbers wiggle, preparing a show,
A talent so grand, even eels want to glow.
Mermaids with mops are cleaning the reef,
While jellyfish giggle, causing comic relief!

There's treasure to find, with a map drawn in cheese,
Where penguins in tuxedos bring everyone to tease.
"Avast ye!" a clam cries, "It's time to set sail!
We'll capture the laughter, it'll never grow stale!"

With each splash and giggle, the tides gently swell,
As all of the ocean begins to rebel.
In a spree of absurdity, we'll laugh till we cry,
Dancing through currents, where silliness flies!

Beneath the Celestial Blue

Under a sky so vast and so wide,
Fish tell tall tales, with great gusto and pride.
A grouper in slippers, oh what a sight!
Said, "Join me for tea, it's a fin-fancy night!"

The starfish are winking, secrets they keep,
"I can't count my arms, but I sure can leap!"
With waves that cover laughter, we swirl and we spin,
Finding fortune in bubbles, let the show begin!

A seaweed magician pulls crabs from a hat,
They march in a line, all dressed up and flat.
"Just one more for luck!" the bubbles do shout,
As the ocean erupts in a comical rout!

From coral cathedrals, the echoes do play,
With jesters in flippers, come join the ballet!
We frolic in humor, beneath azure beams,
Life's just a big joke in our whimsical dreams!

Songs from the Deep

In the heart of the brine, where the fish all reside,
A dolphin with rhythm, he glides with great pride.
"Come dance in the waves, bring your driest old sock,
We'll turn this sea floor into a laughing rock!"

A clownfish is searching for laughs with each fin,
Says, "Knock-knock, who's there? I'm here for a spin!"
With bubbles for beat, and fins all a-flap,
The sea critters join in a lighthearted clap!

In caves made of laughter, they gather and croon,
Singing silly ballads beneath the bright moon.
Geysers of giggles erupting in time,
While the turtles adjudicate beats with a rhyme!

With the tides carrying tunes, we swing and we sway,
Each splash a reminder, make merry today!
From the depths of the blue, our hearts take their leap,
For joy lies within, singing songs from the deep!

Sagas of the Surf

In the frothy wave's embrace,
Laughter bubbles like a race.
Fish in tuxedos, doing the twist,
Dancing with crabs, no chance to resist.

Seagulls squawk in a gossip spree,
Sipping on sea foam, feeling free.
Starfish pose for selfies galore,
Waving at turtles, they beg for more.

Beach balls bounce in a playful row,
Salty breezes join the show.
A dolphin wearing a party hat,
Gives a flip and shouts, "Chat chat!"

Underwater clowns take the stage,
Telling fishy tales with glee and rage.
The ocean's a circus, full of cheer,
And the tide keeps rolling, year after year.

The Call of the Pacific Whisper

In the cradle of tides so wide,
Giggling waves take us for a ride.
A crab with a joke, so witty and sly,
Whispers, "Why don't fish ever fly?"

The sands are soft, the shells like jewels,
Mermaids juggling swimming pools.
Octopuses tangle in the net,
Creating a dance, a whimsical duet.

A surfboard slides like a secret dream,
Sharks wear bow ties and join the scheme.
Gull buddies laugh, 'cause why not yell?
With splashes of joy, they know it well.

Seashells giggle, tickling toes,
They hold the secrets that the ocean knows.
As moonlight winks on the briny bliss,
The sea, oh the sea, cannot be missed!

Echoes in the Deep Blue

Bubbles rise from a bloated seal,
Making faces with the fish, what a deal!
Anemones prance with pink confetti,
They gossip about the ol' mackerel Betty.

Jellyfish glide, all swaying so slick,
They've got moves like they're in a flick.
Clams play cards, oh what a sight,
Under the moon, they play all night.

A dolphin's trumpet fills the sea,
It's the newest hit, can't you see?
Narwhals fish for compliments, so spry,
While sea cucumbers just wonder why.

The ocean floor? A dance party scene,
With conch shells spinning and bubbles keen.
Laughter echoes in hues of blue,
In this aquatic world, where dreams come true!

Odyssey of the Tempest

Stormy skies and a swabby crew,
With rainboots made for a fish or two.
Thunder's laughter shakes the spray,
While squids are dressed for a wild buffet.

A leaky boat, oh what a ride,
As seagulls giggle while trying to glide.
Old sailors tell tales with a wink,
Of mermaids who swim and miss the sink.

The winds are howling, a melody bizarre,
While barnacles play on their rusty guitar.
They strum a tune of the freshest catch,
With a splash here and there, it's quite the match.

In the heart of chaos, joy takes flight,
As fish throw confetti in the pale moonlight.
When tempests roar, we can't help but cheer,
For in wild waters, we find our dear!

The Sea's Heartfelt Saga

In the depths of blue, where fish like to prance,
A jellyfish named Joe loved to dance.
He twirled in the waves, with style so grand,
But bumped into rocks, oh, life's not so bland!

The crabs on the shore laughed at his plight,
Said, "Joe, use your eyes, there's danger in sight!"
But Joe shook his bell, with a grin and a sway,
"I'll jiggle and jangle, come join me today!"

A dolphin swam by, with a wink and a spin,
"Let's host a sea party, where do we begin?"
With bubbles and laughter, they all joined the fun,
A fishy fiesta under the bright sun!

So if you should hear, in the ocean's grand hall,
A giggle or snicker, don't be surprised at all.
For in watery realms where creatures like to play,
There's humor aplenty to brighten your day!

A Symphony of Blue

Bubbles bubble up, and bladders they squeak,
A clownfish conductor making fishy beats.
With seahorses swaying and seaweed in tow,
All marine musicians put on quite the show!

Octopus on drums, with arms all around,
He played a fine rhythm, a strange sounding sound.
The starfish in chorus, they clapped with great glee,
While seagulls above squawked their own harmony!

A turtle chimed in, slow but oh so bright,
"Let's make this a tune that echoes through night!"
With every sea creature, they sang from the heart,
Creating a symphony, a true work of art!

And though it was silly, each note filled with cheer,
The ocean joined in, lending its ear.
So next time you dip your toes in the tide,
Remember the orchestra where laughter resides!

Voyage into Liquid Infinity

On a voyage so wild, with a seal as my mate,
We sailed on a bubble, can you relate?
With a map made of seaweed and dreams in our head,
We sought far-off treasures where fish-like to tread.

A pirate fish yelled, "Arrr, what's your quest?"
"We're hunting for giggles, just doing our best!"
With a swish of his tail, he sent us away,
To wander the vastness, come what may!

Through castles of coral and jungles of kelp,
We stumbled on squids who giggled themselves.
They juggled with shells and performed with great flair,
Leaving us grinning as we danced in mid-air!

At last, as the sun set, our quest came to close,
With laughter and memories, we wouldn't lose.
So if you're adrift, on adventures so free,
Just follow the bubbles, join the fun at sea!

Luminous Legends of the Abyss

In the depths of the dark, an anglerfish glowed,
With a light on her head, just to show off her load.
She gave a sly wink as she waved through the gloom,
"C'mon down for a party, there's plenty of room!"

A deep-sea crab chuckled, his claws all aglow,
"Will we eat fancy shrimp, or just go with the flow?"
With laughter and jests in the blackness so deep,
They spun tales of treasure that made their hearts leap!

Then a pufferfish puffed, bursting with cheer,
"Let's turn this abyss into laughter, my dear!"
With bubbles erupting and giggles galore,
The legends of the deep made quite the uproar!

So if you should venture where the sun fears to creep,
Remember the fun that ignites in the deep.
For in every dark corner, with laughter to brew,
The quirkiest stories are waiting for you!

Beneath the Waves' Whisper

Bubbles rise like tiny jokes,
Making fish giggle in their cloaks.
A crab tells tales with a sideways glance,
While octopuses twist in a silly dance.

Dolphins leap through brighty beams,
Chasing sunbeams, living dreams.
Anemones tickle with wiggly arms,
As sea cucumbers show off their charms.

Starfish play cards on the sandy floor,
While seahorses waltz, what a galore!
The sea's a playground, oh what a scene,
Filled with giggles and all in between.

With playful waves that splash and cheer,
Laughter echoes both far and near.
Under the surface, fun's always alive,
In the ocean's embrace, we all thrive.

The Heart of the Deep Blue

In the depths where shadows prance,
Clownfish giggle, given the chance.
A grouper grins with wide, gappy teeth,
While jellyfish float, quite underneath.

The turtles race in a slow-motion show,
While eager eels twirl below.
A pirate's treasure? Just a lost sock,
Promising laughs on the coral block.

With pufferfish in a worried puff,
Saying, 'This ocean life can be tough!'
But all can agree, though life's quite a hoot,
It's the sea's silly tales that truly suit.

So grab your flippers, let's dive and explore,
Under the waves, you'll never be bored.
In this watery world, joy's the true gem,
Where laughter reigns, and we all stem.

Songs of the Siren's Embrace

Sirens sing with a wink and a smile,
While mermaids play tricks all the while.
With seaweed hair and glittery tails,
They share their secrets in bubbly trails.

One mermaid spat out bubblegum pink,
While others cast nets for a fishy wink.
As seafloor parties bring all the glee,
Their laughter sparks pure jubilee.

The crab DJ spins with claws akimbo,
As starfish dance in a crazy limbo.
"Watch my moves!" the seahorse shouts,
While jellyfish float, checking out clouts.

The ocean's a stage, where antics unfold,
In the warmth of the tide, stories are told.
Dive in, they say, let's chirp and embrace,
For life's a giggle in this magical space.

Tides of Myth and Legend

The tide rolls in, with stories to tell,
Of krakens and cocktails, oh what the shell!
Merfolk exchange tales of lost rubber ducks,
As barnacles chuckle, calling for luck.

A sea monster lounges, sipping his drink,
With a wink he says, 'Life is such a pink!'
Nautical nonsense fills the bright hue,
As squid share secrets, just like a crew.

Bubble parties pop all around,
While sea urchins spin without a sound.
A clam in the corner holds a wild feast,
Celebrating the ocean, to say the least.

So let's raise a fin to the myths of the sea,
With folly and fun, let's just be free.
Join in the laughter, let the ocean gleam,
This whimsical life is the best kind of dream.

www.ingramcontent.com/pod-product-compliance
Lightning Source LLC
Chambersburg PA
CBHW062111280426
43661CB00086B/483